Above the Abyss

Above the Abyss

Emily Isa Danho

VANTAGE PRESS
New York

FIRST EDITION

All rights reserved, including the right of
reproduction in whole or in part in any form.

Copyright © 2003 by Emily Isa Danho

Published by Vantage Press, Inc.
516 West 34th Street, New York, New York 10001

Manufactured in the United States of America
ISBN: 0-533-14251-2

Library of Congress Catalog Card No.: 2002090366

0 9 8 7 6 5 4 3 2 1

Contents

Acknowledgments ix
Author's Note xi
Introduction xiii

Hold onto Your Dreams 1
Land of Democracy 2
Confusion of Men 5
Love, a Grandeur of God 7
Disappearing Professionals 9
My Grandson 10
Those of Different Colors 11
A Call for Justice and Mercy 12
Her Royalty the Cat 13
Life in This Dreamland 14
Love Forever Endures 15
Immoral Living 16
Birth of a Chick 17
Dedicated to the Homeless: Somebody Loves You 18
My Son 19
The Class of 2000 20
To All Senators, Congressmen with All Due Respect 21
A Search for Wisdom 22
The Battle of Black and White 23
Children Bewildered and Lost 24
Equality 25
What Is Man? 26

Memories Erased	27
To Arica, My Little Angel	28
The Valuable Jewel	29
On to the Internet	30
How Soon We Forget	31
The Black Race	32
Love	33
A Faithful Friend	34
My Friends	35
Birth of a New Day	36
To Have a Healthy Heart	37
To All My Children	38
Unwanted at an Old Age	40
Songs of the Rooster	41
Rich and Poor	42
Doctors Are Gifts	43
Mother's Pain of Getting Old	44
To the Old, Lonely, and Forgotten	45
I Have Found Whom My Soul Loveth	46
Our Offspring	47
Young Man	48
Native American	49
Man, a Tower Soon to Fall	50
Yesterdays	51
Restless and Fearful	52
The Backyard Stump	53
Thank You	54
Mother's Love	55
To Those Who Gave Their Life and Love	56
Love Unconditional	57
School of Life	58
My Cat	59
Fearful Times	60
Friendship	61
Living the Fast Life	62
My Nephew	63
Glimpse of Love	64

When I Am Gone	65
Forever I Shall Love Thee	66
To a Special Friend	67
I Am Beautiful Give Me A Chance	68
What Makes One A Star	69
Heros, A Whisper of Good Will	70
Dedicated to All the Lonely and Forgotten	71
Peace and Prosperity?	72
The Boy Elian Gonzales	73
Teaching of Tender Years	74
Man a Shadow Soon to Pass	75
Let Me Do Good	76
Back Then	77
All Is Vanity	79
Vanishing Race	80
To Absorb a Beauty in Life	81

Acknowledgments

After my struggle of years past to complete my book, the satisfaction of completing this is wonderful, for it comes after much pain and pressure and hard work. How wonderful the easing this accomplishment and the relief in the aftermath of its pain. I guarded myself with strength to accomplish that which I thought I could not. I considered, thought, struggled, then I wrote. I am humbled by the strength God gave me. I give special thanks to friends, who gave lovingly of their time to help get my manuscript together.

    Kimberly Boone, for being the covering of my pain;
    Emad Al-Bsi, the pillar of my strength I leaned on;
    John Constantine, for carrying my burden willingly; and
    Diana Contorno and Emy O'Brien, for their labor of love in helping me put my transcript together.

Thanks to all and to all my friends, I love you.

Author's Note

Dear Friends,
 To search one's heart makes for a good thing. It helps us to make the good choices in life. As you do your reading in the evening, and can arouse your judgments, your thinking and your feelings, then I'll know I attained some success in spite of my woes. I don't mean to be ugly, but I must know the truth of things. So as to better our life to be.
 For your patience, your interest and curiosity, I thank you. Critics are invited.
 Thank you.

Introduction

My poems and prose consist of things we don't give thought to. Some may be offending and some pleasing and will open our eyes to our many downfalls. I mean to reveal the other side of human behavior, the natural and careless thoughts, the selfishness and our greedy appetites. Most often we spend our times and energy for things that are void. There are things of more importance in life than money and luxury living.

When you read with open minds, hopefully this will cause you to think of those neglected on the other side of us. And so to better love and care for the poor, the elderly, the maimed and the lonely, the homeless, those hungry, the sick and nature and all creatures. Above all to love and respect all of God's creations. Men have need to learn love and kindness, mercy and justice. Make all equal, no matter the situation, we are all guests on this earth for a little time and a little space in time. Together let's be kind and unselfish. When we pass the time and space on earth, then we leave it all behind and what we did in life will last.

Hold onto Your Dreams

Don't let go of your dreams
My dream I did not let go
Perhaps one day it will come along
Seventy years and I did not give up hope
And still dreaming right on
One day it will come true
Perhaps a dream fulfilled through you
When I wrote those poems and prose
My dream came true
I hope you're pleased when my prose you read
Ignore our handicaps
And hold onto your dream tonight
One day it will come to pass
My schooling was my handicap
At seventy years my hope came to pass
Now my poems and prose I have
Hold on and don't forget
To let your dreams come to pass.

Land of Democracy

They call it the good ol' country
A killing field of the US busy drinking the blood of the innocent
Children kidnapped, raped, killed and left without a trace
Never to be found nor seen again
Families left bewildered, eyes blinded with tears, brokenhearted in a wonder
When a student from a faraway land, in search of his dreams in a dreamland,
Only to have his dream translated into a nightmare land
And be cut off from the face of the earth, by 41 bullets
An only son to his mother, the innocent perish, it's a sad, sad country
When officers become the hoodlums of the streets
With license to carry guns, the innocent to kill and
License to abuse their authority to terrorize the public
When officers have liberty to kill the innocent, of a crime
And then to go in search of a gun to plant at his side
A gun to accuse the innocent of a crime falsely for self-justification
These are men I am supposed to trust with my life
Man perverts that which is right to profit himself
Don't approach me with the good ol' country
When a woman strolling in a park
is approached by men who like wild hyenas
Strip her clothing, harass, rape,
ravish and violate her humanity like wild beasts
While officers of the law stand by to watch
And do nothing to protect the innocent and helpless
When officers act as gangsters and beat a man to a pulp
And leave him for dead,
brain damaged because he has black-colored skin,

For these reasons, justice cries in the streets
When Hollywood is free to teach violence on TV
Molding the innocent young hearts to become violent adults
Hollywood gets rich, while our youth gets fixed
Then expect the parents to wrestle,
control and to clean up Hollywood's mess
It's absolutely a bad country
Man perverts that which is right to profit himself
When cameras are placed in dressing rooms,
in public bathrooms, in hotel rooms.
To watch you bathing, dressing and your private doings
Unrighteousness is a reproach to all nations
When nursing homes neglect,
beat up and rape the helpless elderly, mercilessly
And leaving them lying in their feces, helplessly
These are ones who raised,
cared and built our country for you and for me
This immoral and godforsaken country
When officers get "ticket happy" so to be promoted by it
It's cheating, deceiving, lying and crookery
They run each to his own gain
When the innocent carry guns to kill schoolmates
To commit a crime in school and at home
When a child kills Mom and Dad
When a father can rape his child
When a brother rapes a sister
When a child can't play outside for fear of kidnapping
When you shoot to kill for one's vehicle
When the innocent are under six feet, while their assailants are free
When you burn a place of worship, sacred to man's soul
When one splits a woman's abdomen to steal her unborn
Oh, my, what a world to be in

With this abyss, Hell would be a better place
We have become a perverse and crooked generation
Men, as greedy dogs, look for their own ways
Men has become perverted.

Confusion of Men

We go to the moon in search of the stars
Searching the galaxies, Jupiter and Mars
Can't solve problems on earth we have
Remember Babel? Confused it got
When men become great and knowledgeable
He must needs have a world to rule
He forgets that he is dust, and from whence he comes
The heavens are God's throne
The earth is His footstool, for men to dwell on
Sit yourself on your stool, old men
Constantly we spy on one another
Like thieves in the night, we go warring
To kill helpless, innocent men sleeping
Innocent babe on mother's bosom nursing
United Nations, organization of peace
Has become an instrument of war
By sanctions she causes poverty, hunger, disease to all
We are belly full, children of the world hunger on
We have much, the eye is never full
Never plead the cause of the poor.
With false balance we judge the world
With unrighteous judgments we rule
From her bosom, we snatch her children
To separate fathers from their sons
Forever the state harasses the church
Shifts her responsibility on to the church
To help care for and feed all her poor
Separations intended to keep the state
out of the ruling of the church
Governments twist and turn laws
to suit themselves for gain
Ten Commandments thrown out of schools

Yet, they dare use them in our courtrooms (such hypocrisy)
Our mouths should speak the love of truth and kindness
With all of our knowledge and confusion
Men search the heavens and galaxies to rule
Proverbs 20:24: Man's goings are of God,
how can a man understand his own way.
Isaiah 48:11: "I'll not give my glory to another."
God will not give His glory to men
The moon and the stars to rule
Man's place is at God's footstool.

Love, a Grandeur of God

It comes from the heart of God
As old as eternity and a gift to men
As young as an instant touch of a heart
The instant touch stirs man's innermost being
One becomes embarrassed and blushing
Will not look at the person directly
Wishing only to be in the presence of the other, quietly
The turmoil of love stirs the heart deeply
Love sees all things good, perfect and beautiful
The two begin to take notice of each other's body form
Song of Solomon 7:1–9: How beautiful are thy feet with shoes
The points of thy thighs are like jewels
The work of a cunning workman
Thy navel is like a round goblet which wanteth not liquor
Thy belly is like a heap of wheat set about the lilies
Thy breasts are like two young roes that are twins
Thy neck is as a tower of ivory
Thine eyes like fish pools by the gates of Bethrobim
Thy nose is as a tower of Lebanon pointing towards Damascus
Thy head like Mount Carmel
Thy hair like purple* held in galleries of the kings
Thy stature like a palm tree
Thy breast like a cluster of grapes
So is desire one towards the other
Therefore love endures, hope believes,
Gives, shares, yields and forgives

*Purple was reserved only for the kings.

In its presence there is no fear of death
Jealousy becomes as cruel as graves
The coals are as coals of fire and of vehement flames
at that instant death is present
Therefore, I charge you of the grandeur of God's love
Love explodes in His creation of the world
and of man and mammal alike
Brings two together
For offspring and to create that which become the one
Life created once more again
And again and once more in the face of love
Oh, how wonderful, how pleasant is love, a delight
When love is born, it's pleasingly wonderful, and eternal
And two become one
God's grandeur charged in his creation
Of world man and mammal
Love expelled for eternity to offspring
The one which the two conceive
God's eternal grandeur of love revealed eternally and so it
is.
and the two become one

Disappearing Professionals

Where have our nurses gone
The white cap and her uniforms
Her polished shoes and white hose
Her golden pin on her chest she wore
Representing the school she graduated from
On her graduation she receives
The royal blue cape she wore
Proudly draped over her shoulders to keep warm
Like shining armor standing tall
With a smile taking pride in her profession so
This art of caring for the ailing we've lost
We take no pride in our professions anymore
Nursing now provided by the aiding
Their service overwhelms one with fear and dismay
To them I am just a number
I fear my throat they'll puncture
Service has come down and pricing has gone up
The fear we've undergone
And bills that piled up
We go home sicker, and more problems than before
So man lays and wastes away
"Physician, heal thyself"
I find no diligence nor pride in any profession nowadays
Looking only for the dollar sign and for self gain
Ye are physicians of no value

My Grandson

Grandsons are to love and delight in
Delight and buy him toys to spoil him with
To spend money, to buy him clothes to keep him warm
To laugh with and wipe away all the tears
To feed and make sure of his food to eat, his life to guarantee
To enjoy together a quiet time and story to read
To protect, hug, snug, and sing him to sleep
Wash his face and find a clean spot to kiss
With tender love and care his survival to guarantee
And comfort him when he spills his milk
To worry and lose sleep when he is sick
His problems and worries make my life complete
And so I delight in showing off my child's offspring
The flower of my home
The olive branch on my table
Tata loves you, my grandson
My joy, my love, my happiness, my delight
My roots, my offspring.

Those of Different Colors

Men judge me by the color of my skin
I am hated, accused, slugged, beaten for the color of my skin
I am abused, arrested, dragged, lynched for the color of my skin
I did not choose Mom and Dad
I chose not the color black
I had nothing to do with that
Before I was conceived, God saw me as that
My members were brought together by God like that
My spirit given me as yours, white man
Don't look at me through your eyes
Look at me through your heart
Enable me, the chance you have to live and love
That I may learn to love you just as you are
We are both a part of God's Spirit
A just and humble one must see through his heart
Forgive me for expressing myself freely
I am the handiwork of God.

A Call for Justice and Mercy

A man condemned taken to trial.
The animal in us begins to rise.
A man broken as he stands
No one hears "innocent" he cries.

As buzzards go after a carcass
We, as wild dogs, tear his life apart.
His character, life and name destroyed.
His job taken away from him.
Family members torn apart.
Children. loved ones now are gone.
Distressed and haunted—so he stands.
Justice and mercy now, he cries.
Justice and mercy does not hear.

Brokenhearted now he is,
Broken-spirited and dismayed.
We seem to forget the human pain.
The name justice we've destroyed.
He could very well be innocent you know.
So justice and mercy are not found.

Her Royalty the Cat

Like a queen, my home she rules
Stares at my face my thoughts to know
Noble as royalties are her demands
Roams my home all day and all night
Guarding the house from the criminal mouse
One hardly notices she is around
With soft and gentle purr she speaks
As though to say "Sardines, please"
So keen the sound of her ears
She catches her prey with perfect ease
Ancient people thought her a god
Her quiet and mysterious way earned her that
As quiet as a mouse she sleeps on her mat
In the living room she takes her bath
She prefers the company of the old
Together they snooze and lazy on
She brings comfort to lonely hearts
They murmur their discomfort and pain
She sings and purrs her quiet meows
Her gentle ways and starry eyes
Makes her company much desired
Plays the strings and tosses it about
Quietly plays and lays on her back
And so put out at night
To catch her runaway rat.

Life in This Dreamland

The fabric of our family and society is falling apart
Our children growing without a family bond
They are falling between the cracks
We're taking away the sunshine from their home life
Proverb: 29:15: A child left to himself bringeth his mother to shame
The family are torn apart
They look to back alley, a friend to find
The high cost of living brought it about
It takes two working to make it out
To have to fill a house and get the car
Therefore we labor day and night
Supporting a family the county, city, and government
the bills never stop, the sooner you pay one, another comes around
Tomatoes come gassed and with a great price
Wilted vegetables cost so much
Fruits are picked green, just don't taste right
Beef sticks as tough as the sole of a shad
Hollywood takes over to raise the child
With violence and crimes carving their hearts
Expecting the family to clean up their mess
Proverbs: 17:13: Whose regardeth evil for good.
Evil shall not depart from his house
We've been made accustomed to make
Big ruckus over nothing
We make big ruckus over material things, wealth and money
With this process, our family separated, neglected and forgotten
Proverbs: 23:4: Labor not to be rich, cease from thine own wisdom.

Love Forever Endures

When love is born in the heart of men
The expression embodies a secret feeling
Its secrecy becomes overwhelming
It's read through the eyes and facial expressions
When it's intertwined love becomes of one heart
When in each other's presence, in heaven they stand
Love accepts each other with all their faults
As we accept the rose with her thorns
Love accepts as is and covers all sins
In the presence of love death is not feared
And will comfortably embrace her
For love is as strong as death
And jealousy becomes as cruel as a grave
Generations come and generations go
Cities change and countries erase to become without a trace
Love endures and forever will stand and not change
Without love man is a sound of brass and a tinkle of the cymbal
Many waters cannot quench love
Neither can the floods drown it.
Love radiated in the grandeur
of His creation of the world and us.

Immoral Living

We're living in fearful times
A world turning upside down
Homosexuals and lesbians
Rubbing our nose to the ground
In the closets they were hiding
They must have known 'twas not right
Amorality on the rampage
Nude women everywhere
When raped, wolf they cry
Police officers, untrustworthy
They kill and accuse innocents falsely
There is no integrity to judge righteously
Our children disappearing every day
Most are never found
A thought comes to mind
Organ you suppose?
We gave ourselves to lasciviousness
And the lust of the flesh
Favor is deceitful and beauty is vain
One having integrity and morals
Honor and praise will follow

Birth of a Chick

A chick pops her head out
And proceeds from her egg
She looks to the right
She sees hunger, poverty and street living
She turns to her left
She sees violence, gangs and immorality
She looks ahead
She sees war, death and the innocent dying
She looks to her back
She sees distress of nations and suffering
She looks up to the sky
She sees bomb shells falling
She looks down to her feet
She sees hell and brimstone
She becomes nervous, fearful and discontent
And says this world is not for me
I won't be passing through
Heaven, please open your doors
I wish no part of it all
Said good-bye and proceeded back to her shell
And a whisper, life overwhelming and unending troubles

Dedicated to the Homeless: Somebody Loves You

When I was born scrawny, ruddy and wrinkled.
From the air came a whisper how beautiful
I grew up unattractive with beauty undesired
Bills I could not pay
Work I could not find
I sat, wished, hoped, and gazed
In misery and loneliness I bathed
I became homeless and poor
In the streets, begging for food
Holding the cup, hoping for change
Seems no one cared to look
Help was nowhere
My condition turned one's head
In my state I am comforted,
For I know there is one from her innermost being
Forever her arms open wide for me
Has love, care and compassion for me
Mama loves me unconditionally
Man born of a woman is
of few days and full of troubles
Here, a moment in time
Please, to me be kind.

My Son

My son, I love you morning and nights
My love for you is unconditional
I wish for you the good and bright future,
to live and walk it in its fullest
The road ahead is rough and you'll walk it alone
I'll not be there to hold your hand
Be strong, be wise, count your days and walk upright
My son, turn the wrong to that which is right
I wish for you to be adorned with meek and quiet spirit
Determined to show love and not hate
Let your words be few, be not hasty with your heart,
buy truth, and sell it not
I wish for you to judge your way righteously
To seek God's wisdom and understanding,
To seek knowledge and the fear of God
Above all, to search for them as hidden treasures
Then you'll know the fear of God and awake in his
likeness
And so to bathe your hands in innocence
Make good use of your God-given days
for the moment in time will soon be here
The break of dawn and the morning sun
will pass and no longer be seen
You'll go to your long home
to be remembered no more
What you do in your life for God and man,
this only shall last
My son, if you keep God's word
and hide them in your heart,
Then, you shall have good success.

The Class of 2000

Wishing for your success now that you've arrived to face life
Life is a raging sea filled with turmoils, tears and fears
You labor to make it, for life gives nothing free
Alone you won't exist, working with others it must be
To get along give a kind word, gentle smile,
and be of quiet spirit
Your days are few and full of troubles to boot
Fighting and disagreeing with men is cowardly
To be hasty with words is unwisely
There be more hope in a fool than thee
For a fool speaketh his mind,
but the wise keepeth it to himself
Sweet talk will bring out the snake from her den
And is like chaff blowing in the wind
For out of the heart men speak
Speak truth sooner or later it will surface
And the heart it will pierce
Meet life with wisdom, truth, gentle quiet spirit,
humility and understanding
Seek wisdom and the fear of God above knowledge
Then you shall have good success
Keep your heart with all diligence,
for out of it comes the essence of life.

To All Senators, Congressmen with All Due Respect

How low can a man get for revenge?
To expose his sin to the world on the Internet
A man and a country has been shamed
A punishment too great to bear
Such punishment is quite enough
Please dismiss this case tonight
This nation does not want to hear
Intelligent men beggaring still
No one seems to want to agree
Perhaps because we all have sinned
Why don't you search for Mister Mercy
And forgive that ye may be forgiven
Please spare him the stars tonight
Perhaps we're too righteous that we cannot
Too much suffering has been done
Lay it down and leave it to God
It takes one to be blunt
For another to understand.
Forgive me if I am offending
I just love Mr. Mercy

A Search for Wisdom

Money, we wish we have it
Wealth, we like to grab hold of it
Fun and pleasure, we give into it
Love, we yearn for it
Knowledge, we wish to have it
When death knocks we yield to it
Wisdom, we search not for it
Get wisdom, get understanding
Embrace her, she will crown you
With her honor, her glory, her grace
In all our getting
Wisdom is forgotten.

The Battle of Black and White

All men are created equal
Yet unequal for the skin-toned men
The skin-toned has no voice nor rights
Still slaving for the benefits of the whites
The blond hair and the blue eyes
All come from faraway lands
Looking for their dream in the new land
A dream most will never find
For some the dreamland becomes
their nightmare land
Their sin is the color of their skin
They'll get knocked around a bit
And taken advantage of a little
The role of race continues on in peaceful times
And we accept it and turn a blind eye
Whites always suspicious of blacks
And never give the benefit of the doubt.
A world unequal to all ethnic backgrounds
All ethnics treated with a little less respect
We must learn to love and respect
all men as they come
If it's possible to live peaceably with all men
Man's going is of God
How can He understand his own ways?
Exod. 22:21 "Thou shalt not vex a stranger, nor oppress him, for ye were a stranger in the land of Egypt."

Children Bewildered and Lost

What's happening to our children today?
Working mothers have gone away,
Mothers busy from day to day,
Working, laboring for tomorrow's pay.

Tender mother's touch has disappeared
We leave our children with fear,
Her tender care no longer there.
Our children left in others' care,
Holding a key to an empty house,
Roaming the streets, looking for love.

Yesterday her love was near.
Her gentle hand was here to lead.
The look in her eyes with love was filled,
Her tender heart no longer near.
I look to bond with strangers near,
Those who roam the streets.
Mother gathering her worldly wealth,
And lost her children's love.

Equality

I am judged by the color of my skin
For the face I carry
For the length and shortness of my body
For my ethnicality, language, wealth and poverty
My culture, customs and nationality
For my cuisine and the way I eat
My religion and my beliefs
And the ancient garb I wear
Must I do away with my ancient culture
And be forced to accept white men's ways?
Must I erase the ways and memories of my ancestry?
Must I forget custom, culture, language, and nationality,
Assuming I have no culture or background
to be an American,
For to be intertwined and accepted
one with white man
This will forever be a thorn in the flesh
For all men are one and created equal,
in spite of race, culture, or nationality
It is man who determines his equality
Love accepts all as is and covers all sin.

What Is Man?

What is man that You are mindful of him?
Man unable to rule and lead his home
Unable to control, guide and lead his children at home
Yet, he must needs to rule a world
He forgets that he is clay
He crouches as bold as a lion
To run, to catch, to devour his prey
To take of the world his heart's desire
Without mercy at any price
He wishes to rule the world with iron hand
And get what he wants of the world's wealth
Born of a woman, his birth like the birth of the beasts of the fields
His days shadowed few in number
And swiftly passing
He thinks himself to be a god,
trying to reach a universe and rule the skies
He forgets that he is dust
Man is worm, his breath in his nostrils
His pride, his name, his strength's vain
Man rages and imagines vain things
Should he be magnified and made high?
His is the flower which blooms and fades away
Man is grass, his days of shadows, swiftly passing
Man is worm.
Job 24:20: The womb shall forget him. The worm shall feed sweetly
on him and he shall be no more remembered.

Memories Erased

I went back to where I grew up
Our house I could not find
Where I stood I did not know
Friends and neighbors are all gone
Memories erased away
A place left with no story to tell
Of those who were living there
All gone and all is farewell
Innocent and naive we seemed to be
We think forever things will be
The slightest breath of wind will be gone
All is forgotten, with the wind it's blown
No story or memories of us to tell
Ruins and broken homes of war, all that remains
Seems never one was there
Seems my world was never there.

To Arica, My Little Angel

You are an angel
Angels are sent from God
To heal and cheer broken hearts
You are as precious as that
To share your best with me (that night)
You are better than angels, to share your best with strangers
Because you have done that, I love you more tonight
You, the angel in disguise
You are God's love sent from above
Please accept this gift
It is my way of saying thanks a bit
It is people like you
Who make the world worth living in.

The Valuable Jewel

The beauty of marble in its polishing
The beauty of gold in its refining
The beauty of a diamond in its pressuring
The beauty of gems is in their polishing and grinding
When light reflects their inner beauty is seen
The beauty of child in his correction
Correction of a child is as carving a stone
The beauty of the old is in their hard knocks
in life experiences
And the honor of the old man is his gray hair
As a diamond is a chunk of coal
made good under pressure
So does a child make good under correction.

On to the Internet

"Jealousy is cruel as the graves" S of S 8:6
To the world on the Internet
A laughing stock to the world we have become
A group of educated men so called
Forgetting where they came from
Believing they are innocent, one and all
As children bickering together still
We must justice and mercy call
We must get rid of the mess Star caused
To forgive a man seems hard
Perhaps we are righteous that we cannot
Such problems seems we cannot solve
It seems we complicate things more
A fallen star is too much to bear
Left her crevice on Washington there
We have been shamed in the presence of the world.
Judge not that ye not be judged
And complete this circus round.

How Soon We Forget

Easter Sunday morning
Good people go to worship
Remembering Christ has risen
The rest of the year forgetting Christ is near
Until Christmas again on the scene appears
We rush to celebrate with gifts for ourselves to bring
Christ is born, his life on the Cross, for men he gave
The gift of redemption to men he brings
A gift of life to man he has given
Some remember faithfully
Some remember selfishly
Till the next year
For now it's all forgotten.

The Black Race

You came to my land
By force and violence
Carried me away from family, home and loved ones
You shackled my feet and hands
Across the seas you took me away from husbands,
children and wives
I labored for you day and night
To till your earth and build your house
My labor came without a price
Often times innocent, but was accused of crimes
And took me out on a tree to hang
Those of my race which survived, were stripped of all
their rights
And separated from whites
Today I am accused and arrested by my profile
And I am still not sure I will survive
For your police brutality has the upper hand
I waited patiently for my chance to come
I was cut down, but I came forth like a flower
Free at last
Thank God, my cry reached the heavens
Thank God, now I am free

Love

From birth a baby looks for love
Man goes to his grave yearning for love
He lives searching for love
One is withdrawn when not certain of love
You die when you lose your love
A heart bubbles with joy when love is found
Love, the essence of security and life
It brings satisfaction
The essence of joyful living
To be present with ones you love
When love is near, fear of death disappears
When love is gone, a home is destroyed
And loved ones are torn apart
It will bring death, gloom and destruction
When love is found
To all our faults is blind
We are born, we live, we die yearning
And searching for love
"Love is strong as death
Much water cannot quench love
Neither can the floods drown it." Song of Solomon: 8:7

A Faithful Friend

Friends are of value, you can't find every day.
They come to your aid when you need help
They don't cast you away when you make mistakes.
They'll stand by you when you're depressed.
When the world is against you,
they comfort when you are suppressed.
When you fall, they hold you up and give you aid.
Friends remain steadfast all the days
And stick with you through thick and thin, always.
They hold a bond and respect for you they maintain
It's a lifetime investment: so precious,
They are not made in one day.
They weep and miss you when you pass away.
Hold onto them—they are scarce and they are priceless.
You don't find one every day.

My Friends

It takes one to be blunt
For the other to understand
Perhaps I am too blunt, I know you will forgive
Writing was an ordeal to wrestle with
And a tall mountain to climb
With no intentions of hurting anyone's heart
I wrestled and did my best to get it down
My arrangements of wordings may not be right
So I beg your pardon for that
I hope you'll enjoy this book for now
And I'll try harder for the next time around
I hope you'll enjoy reading and be blessed
By reading the hope is to get better through life
With our children, family, friends and government
You may find my writing blunt and rough at times
However it's the truth and truth hurts,
Wounds and pierces the heart
For morality, integrity, and justice are our best assets
May God bless you tonight
And thank you so very much.
Let's gird ourselves with wisdom and strength
To do that otherwise we can't.

Birth of a New Day

Silent and sleepy world awakens at the break of dawn
Like the woman with birth pains,
Giving birth to her new day
From a distance a rooster crows announcing
To the world a birth of the new day
Cool breeze sweeps across my face
The fragrance of jasmine in the air
A floating hummingbird in
search of a flower for her honey
The sound of a woodpecker,
stamping his mark on a tree bark
A squirrel scratching in search of her nut
Bees and butterflies dancing in the air
The casual passing of a cat
A bark of a dog from a distance
The passing of a motor vehicle,
disturbing the music of the early dawn
Then suddenly a burst of sun rays on the horizon
The hawk cries at the bursting of the sun
Introducing the birth of her new day
The day is born, snoring fathers awakened
Mothers and children yawning, stirring
The world alive and all its commotion
going until the final hours of a day
The sun disappears and dusk appears
And darkness is ever near
Darkness overwhelms and comes to claim her day
The world sleeps, a day disappears, never to reappear
The rooster's morning crow of praise now silent
A day forever gone
Finally, a moment in time is past.

To Have a Healthy Heart

Bend and help a hungry soul
Give and it shall be given to you
The measure you give shall be given back to your bosom
Don't fear your yesterday's mistakes
Yesterday was your former day,
they are now of old
A lesson learned
Let's look for today,
the new beginning to make it better
Don't worry about your tomorrow's uncertainties
Tomorrow will care for itself and will provide its daily bread
Have no fear when you foresee your storms
Your faith will see God and God will still your storm
If you believe in eternity,
your better days are ahead
And today's problems are of no worry,
they shall pass away
Believe in God, He will see you through
Keep a tender, loving,
and compassionate heart towards all
It will come back to you.

To All My Children

Yesterday you were the flower bud in my home
Today you opened up into a beautiful bloom,
Perfumed with personality, beauty, strength and maturity
Now you are the dancing bee in the home of your mom
    and dad
Tomorrow you'll become an executive, doctor,
senator, perhaps a president and maybe a garbage man
Nothing is wrong with that, all are little jobs for the
    moment in time
When you get there,
I'll brace my back to remember our good times past
Remember the coffee times we used to have?
When you broke my cookie jug,
When Mom and Dad came to pick you up, under my table
    you'd hide,
When you put the roll of tissue down my commode,
When you were happy to see the milkmaid come,
When you sneaked out to play in the backyard,
When I changed your diaper and you showered me with
    it,
When you locked me out of my house,
When you did your art work with your BM on my walls,
Then completed the art work with crayons on my
    furniture and floors,
When your screams reached the Atlantic,
When your aroma filled my house and I had to give you a
    bath,
When you chased my pet chicken trying to lay her egg,
When two lambs went skipping across my yard
innocently, one of human, the other of livestock.
When you cried, I told you to sit and cry,
but make it quiet—babies asleep

You sat, lowered your voice, like a good boy
When four of you took my loaf of bread to eat,
I walked in and your hands and mouth stuffed with it,
it revealed your sin
When I saw the look in your eyes and face,
I had no choice but your sin to forgive
You ruled my home with your innocent times,
I wish those days were forever
You were the olive branches around my house
You are the heritage of God, you filled my quiver
You bring such good memories of my past,
Because of you, my life is full and I am blessed
Children are arrows in the hand of the mighty
You spiced my life with your good humor
and memories to cherish,
The beauty of your innocence unequaled,
my children, I love you so much
Unless we become little children in spirit
we cannot see the kingdom of God,
We shall not enter, nor inherit, God's kingdom,
Let the children come, of such is the kingdom
Nursey
Mama Peaden
Mama Daniel
Tata

Unwanted at an Old Age
(Dedicated to all the elderly placed in nursing homes)

Once love was giving and was not forgotten
My children care not for me today
I became a burden to them in my age
Checking for a nursing home to place me there
I gave and spent a lifetime of worry and care
They'll not give one year of their time for me
In the nursing home placed and forgotten me
Against my will and my home and life's dreams
Thus they took all rights from me
I am stripped of home, privacy, sentiments, and life
My dream of the past and joyful memories erased
Of my privacy, dignity, pride and right, I am stripped
forced to give in to other's demands
Yielding under the care of those who love me not
A life of love and care wasted away and forgotten
My reward humbled and brokenhearted I stand
Once a year they check me out
Perhaps wishing I died somehow
In reality a relief to them if I disappeared
And so be free of burden and worry of me
In my eyes, a disgrace to get rid of parents
Who gave of perfect love to bring you up
Putting a parent away, should never come to that
For where there is true love,
Love will prevail, for love is as strong as death
The old are the blessings in a home.
Lev. 19:32: "Thou shalt rise up before the hoary head,
And honor the face of the old man and
fear the God, I am the Lord."

Songs of the Rooster

From the break of dawn and the bursting of the sun
Faithfully the rooster cries out his praise,
"Cock-a-doodle-do"
Praising God for his new day and food
So does the chirping of the birds
And the budding of the flower in her morning dew
Her face toward the heavens
Petals open wide, facing upward to the sky
With her praise to God
So does the rooster's "Cock-a-doodle-do"
To God, his creator his praise to do
Does more than human should do
Man seems to forget his creator
His knowledge his deceiver
Men thinking only of his cup of coffee
"Let everything that hath breath praise the Lord"
The rooster his praise will not forget
Man seems always his maker to forget
Man's breath in his nostrils
What is man to be accounted of?

Rich and Poor

Some have it all, some have none at all
Those who have none labor for naught
Those who have will labor not
The rich play and the poor gaze
The rich bathe in luxury
The poor bathe in misery
Wealth makes many friends
The poor separated from men
Wealth makes fame
Poverty forgets one is there
All run to help the rich in hopes to gain a bit
The cause of the poor no one pleads
The poor cry and no one hears
The rich, belly full, the poor hunger on
The rich, all wish to rub shoulders with
The poor, afflicted and men abhor them
The rich and the poor meet together
God the maker of them both
Empty-handed we come, empty-handed we go
Proverbs 29:8: Give me neither poverty nor riches
Feed me food convenient for me,
Lest I be full and deny thee,
And say, "Who is the Lord?"
Or lest I be poor and steal and take the name of God in vain.

Doctors Are Gifts

Doctors are gifts to men
Without which will not survive
We pray God to guide their healing hands
A gift of life so great to have
A gift of sight none to compare
Without eyesight darkness reigns
We thank you for giving us hope
The blooming flowers and the rose to behold
With birds and butterflies floating about
And so to enjoy all colors in sight
The piercing rays of golden sun
And God's handiwork of the early dawn
We thank you so very much
Ever grateful the work of your hand.

Mother's Pain of Getting Old

When I get old, children rush to take control
To the nursing home they send me
There you are cared for, they tell me
Of my freedom and independence they strip me
In other's care they leave me
Like vultures they make speed my spoil to divide
Like buzzards, my sentimentals
and possessions to grab
My home they sell,
never to set foot in it again
All memories and sentiment erased
All my love and years of labor wasted away
Left with those who have no love for me
Under their demand and mercy helplessly
In the darkest hour,
God knows what they'll do to me
My lifetime's investment and
love torn apart in one might
With tender love to my children I labored to give
My reward a castaway to be
As I watch my nest torn apart from under my feet
Great pains grab my heart
I give my heart to my children
My children's heart to the rocks.

To the Old, Lonely, and Forgotten

When I get old, fear begins to overtake me
I ask myself, will my children care for me?
Will they place me in others' care
Where love for me does not reign?
Will they care to visit me there?
Will they forget that I am there?
My belongings they will divide and sell
The money they will pocket for gain
Memories erased, before my eyes, which once were there
Life will be forced out of me then
Children have no love for parents
Like the love we had and gave yesterday.

I Have Found Whom My Soul Loveth

I found her whom my soul loveth
Rise up come away with me
Let me hear thy voice
Your love is enchanting
Filling my heart with secrecy
You're ravishing my heart from within
Stirring my innermost being
My desire is towards thee
In your presence, in heaven I stand
How fair is your love towards me?
Draw me, we will run after thee
We will be glad and rejoice in thee
I will love thee with an upright love
I shall keep thy comings and thy goings
From this time forth and forever I shall love thee
Song of Solomon : 2:4: He brought me to the banqueting house,
His banner over me was love.

Our Offspring

Mother's womb is a flowering garden
It brings forth children, fun and laughter
Spreading our roots through the world's gardens
Each bloom perfumed with various size,
Colors of personalities and actors
Filling a world with different hues,
shapes, sizes and faces.
Keeping alive our genes,
as chain of ringlets
The flowering branches to our generation ever after
And so to make the sunshine
in our life brighter
To continue to bring love, joy,
and happiness ever after
I am fearfully and wonderfully made.
My substance was not hid from thee.
When I was made in secret and curiously wrought
in the lowest part of the earth.

Young Man

Young man, be joyful in thy youth
Eat, drink, be merry
But without abuse
For gray hair lies at your door
Those who were before are forever gone
Be assured that death will knock at your door
You will forever be gone as those before
"Remember thy creator in the day of thy youth"
While the evil days come not
Nor the years drove night
When you shall say I have no pleasure in them
Young man, walk in the way of good men
And keep the faith of righteousness
Proverbs 2:20: "For length of days and
long life and peace shall they add to thee."

Native American

Once land and buffalo rich
Now the country's poorest exist
I call for my right to manage my land
My timber, my oil, what's left of mine
White man focused his eye and stealing me blind
White men's wall of promises don't stand
Its mortar made of greed, deceit, and lies
One promise made true, my land he took
In the name of God from a faraway land
He came, he took my blood
He ravished and he took my land
Now his eyes focus on what's left of mine
My timber and my oil
Full of greed, he stops at nothing
He only trusts in the God of his money
He sold his God for the God of his buck
I, a wounded doe, am sure for the slaughter to vanish
I grieve for you, my friends, life does not fair.
We've become like greedy dogs, which never have enough
Warring man's feet run to evil
Spreading a net lying in the wait
So are the ways of the greedy men
Which taketh away man's life to gain.

Man, a Tower Soon to Fall

Man thinks himself forever to be
Gives not a thought of what tomorrow will bring
He rules a world as he sees fit.
A strong tower forever to be
Holds his head high and speaks his piece
Only to crumble and stoop on his feet.
One must hold His hand to lead
For stooped and feeble he is
A tower at last too feeble to stand
One must give him a helping hand
So he stands one foot in his grave
and one on the ground.
A man like the blooming flower, soon he falls
So he falls to his grave and off his feet.
Forever forgotten, sad it is
Man's breath in his nostril
Wherein is he to be accounted of?

Yesterdays

Mothers, children, and our working dads
We've lost our good simple life
With our clothes swaying on the lines
Mother staying home with her child
Cooking and smelling the aromas and satisfied
Sitting out in screen-covered porches in summer heat
Waiting, looking for her hard-working man
Divorce was not the thing of the past
Dysfunctional family we did not have
Yesterday families were a valuable prize
Too expensive today to come by
We had no cooling, heating, nor today's conveniences
Happy we were at that and satisfied
We had our children whom we loved
Were secure, we didn't ask for much
Our time spent with family and friends
We were completely satisfied
We found wisdom from yesterdays, experiences past
Be old fashioned and bring back our past
Those days were like unique antiques and a valuable prize
Come, my friends, don't discard us
You'll learn more about life from us
We found wisdom by experiences of our past.

Restless and Fearful

When I go to school each day
I get restless now and then
For I know when I go home
Mom and Dad will not be there
When I get out of school
I go home to an empty house
I get scared of a stranger around
I hold the key in my hand
And say a prayer, please God
Protect and be with me tonight
Till Mom arrives with Dad
When Mom comes, the feelings change
Love, protection is everywhere
'Til the break of day is here again

The Backyard Stump

Too deep to uproot and ugly to look at
Full of bugs and ants so undesired
Stuck up in my yard like a sore thumb
I wish to remove it but couldn't do so
I stared at it every day or so
I have learned to ignore it so
I wondered what to do with it now
I dug around and flowers did plant
Tomorrow the sun will shine
The daffodils will bloom in the sun
The wind will blow, the daffodils will dance with the breeze
The ivy will grow and cover that ugly stump
Then, around the stump I'll smile and chat
Covered with flowers and ivy around
To solve your daily stump, plant your flowers around
To solve your daily care
Plant your flowers here and there
And around the stump you will sit and rest.

Thank You

To those giving of their time lovingly,
I wish to say Thank You
for everything you do.
Labor of love you have shown
Reveals God's love in you.
Silently you've labored arduously
Did so with open arms.
Like the flower blooming in secrecy
With the bursting of the morning sun
Revealing its beauty
So does the labor of your hands
Silently, patiently, and lovingly you've labored on.
So once more I wish to say thank you
And I thank God for you.

Mother's Love

When Mother's heart is hard like a rock
God help the child under her hand
Her home should be filled with love
Instead it's filled with fear and doubt
A home where security should reign
Fear, tears, and dismay are there
I sit in the corner of the court yard all day
While my heart gets harder towards her
I ran away from home
Trying to get away from her
And hope she'll forget me some way
When a home is not filled with love
It becomes worse than Hell inside
Everything I do is never right
And constantly criticized
I sat in a corner all day
And wished and prayed I'd die some way
Now I harbor only hate for her
When I grew up to a young lady
I could not say the word "Mommy"
Love your children not with toys nor clothes
Love them genuinely
Childhood love won't be retrieved
Nothing compares or takes the place of love.
Love is strong as death.

To Those Who Gave Their Life and Love

When you grow like a tower, and become
as beautiful as a flower,
Will you love me?
When you get older and strong
to become as the rose in a garden
And I get old and become wrinkled as a prune,
Will you still love me?
When my eyes grow dim and cannot see,
Will you hold my hand and lead me?
When Alzheimer's strikes and I am helpless as a child
Will you leave me in other's care, and forget I am there
When I get there you will wish me gone
Will you still love me?

Love Unconditional

Mother's love, the nearest thing to God's love
She gives of herself and her life to her child
With gentleness she nourishes her children
Patiently she guides and leads them
Her hand is kindness and teacher of grace
Always ready to forgive and forget
Her love and forgiving heart,
As far as heaven and earth apart
Her tenderness, the cool breeze of heaven
Love absolute, invisible, untouchable
Encircles to grip deep within her soul,
Is as deep as the abyss
Love never changes and ever stands
In death, in life, in sorrow, always the same
The twinkle of love revealed through her eyes
In poverty, with tenderness
Removes her morsel to feed her child
Love gripped deep in her soul,
To vanish only in her death
And the womb will remember it no more.

School of Life

I grew up with no schooling to speak of
Graduated from college,
thought I knew it all.
Holding certificate,
I spoke with pride and bounce to show
Only to discover
how much I did not know.
I have learned nothing I realized.
This School of Life
I have just begun.
Experience of life teaches one all. . . .
The school you don't graduate from.
Seventy years, still going strong
However older, but wiser now.
I look at life with a different eye,
So now I give wisdom a try.
Coupled with humility and understand now,
Life challenges
with wisdom to comfort
I put arrogance and pride aside
For discretion preserves me
Understanding will keep me
My life with wisdom I perceive
With humility to others, I speak
As I travel to arrive at that moment in time
Life's teaching
will not present a certificate to me.
Proverbs 4: Wisdom is the principal thing. . . .
Embrace her, she shall promote thee,
Exalt her, she shall bring thee to honor
She shall deliver a crown of glory
And give to thy head an ornament of grace.

My Cat

Mysterious cat roaming around my house
Her gentle paws silently,
trotting all over the place
Staring at the moon,
which followed there
She sat in a curl and stared at it then
She caught with her eye
an owl on a branch
Wondering how she could
bring him down
Along appears a mouse
to come out to play
And steers the cat's attention away
She chased after him
but he got away
So she resigned with creeping things to play
Till the break of dawn and the morning sun
To the back door
she runs to sing her meows
As though to say "my tuna now"
Filling her belly then stares
at my face much obliged
Walking away tail upward and so dignified
Resigning to her mat
To take her nap,
following her bath
Quiet please! Hmm hmm, what a night
Well, the haughtiness of a cat
shall be brought down.

Fearful Times

We're living in fearful times
A world turning upside down
Divorce is ever high
Children shuffled to and from, between parents
In courts endless fighting for support
Insecurity in children we mold
Immorality on the rampage
Nude women everywhere
Let their boobs hang out
Wear rope between their buns
When raped, wolf, she cries
Homosexuals and lesbians
Walking after their lust
In their closets they were hiding
Must have known it 'twas not right
Out of closets now are crawling
To defile those who are not
forcing a world to think it's right
We gave ourselves to lasciviousness and the lust of the flesh
As was in the day of Sodom and Gomorrah
Romans 1:26–27: "Women did change the natural use into that
which is against nature.
Likewise, men leaning the
natural use of women burned in their lust one toward another
Man with men working that
which is unseemly, receiving to
themselves that recompense
of their error which was meet."

Friendship

Friends are expensive and bard to find
They are precious things to have
They are the sun in a garden never fading in our lives
For better or for worse the friends you always trust
The caring never changes or subsides
The quality of a newborn's beauty is tenderness and love
All beauty changes with time
Beauty of friendship that always lasts
We are glad when they come to our life
The longer friends, the greater the bond we'll have
They make the garden in our life bloom after the rain
Their inner beauty for ever is there
In life we all need them and are poor without them
Friends are what makes a heart glad.

Living the Fast Life

Life of a dreamland
Life so complex, like the raging sea
It keeps one on edge
Have no time for family
Have no time for friends
Nor time for one's self
No quality time for children
Left to roost in day care
Running to and fro each day
Working my life away to meet up with my bills
In a blinking eye. I am turning to gray
My life slipping away, racing the loot to make
Paying my tax, insurance, interest and compiled bills
I look through a glass darkly to see how I have aged
I did the best I could and gathered all sorts of goods and loot
And so now to bid it all farewell
Under the sun man labors for the mind
To leave it all behind
Man in every way as he comes, so he shall go.
With open band he is born, with open band he goeth.
Ec:3: "What profit hath a man of all his labor
Which he taketh under the sun."

My Nephew

Your face is the sunshine on a cloudy day
You're the cool breeze, from heaven sent
The breath of air which fills a heart with love
In you I see the gentle, meek, and quiet spirit of God
The moment in time you have on earth
'Twill be the blessing to us all
May God make you a blessing
to all those who cross your path
I give thanks to the One who brought
all things into existence
And keeps the heavens in place
God bless and keep you all day and all night
Under His watchful eye
I love you very much.

Glimpse of Love

Father and child bidding each other good-bye
Arms wrapped around each other in a clinch so tight
For a moment both refusing to let go
I observed a strong bond between them both
As she entered her vehicle to depart
From a distance, Dad waved,
And kept waving his hand until the vehicle rounded the corner
And faded out of sight and disappeared
Dad still waving in hopes she caught
A glimpse of the wave of his hand
At that instant my dad comes to mind
Wishing he were around
I am not as lucky as that
Instant tears filled and drowned my eyes
Wishing him here to share a bond we once had
To wrap my arms around him and clinch to him so tight
Dad was taken from me
Years of our life stolen from him and me
I was deprived of him, left with love unexpressed
Death lay claim to him
My heart is silenced
I see others love and clinch
I stand looking wishing with tears
Wishing for those lost years
For I know 'twill never be.

When I Am Gone

Life gives one a trembling heart
A failing of sight and sorrow of mind
And a wonder of assurance of life
When I am gone
Don't grieve for me,
In His presence I'll stand
His face I'll see
His hand in mine
Leading me to the promised land.
In Him I'll be satisfied
Then I'll shimmer like the stars
For He is the bright and morning star
A new body he'll give me
To match the heavenly
I'll thank God I'll be free.

Forever I Shall Love Thee

I found her whom my soul loveth
The turmoil of your love stirs my heart deeply
In your presence, in heaven I stand
My desire is towards thee
In your face I have no fear of death
Rise up, come away with me
Let me hear your voice
Your love is enchanting
Filling my heart with secrecy
You ravish my heart from within
How fair is your love towards me
Choose me. I will run after thee
I will love thee with an upright love
From this time forth and forever
I shall love thee.

To a Special Friend

You're the friend one wishes for,
Without which, one cannot afford.
You reveal God's love to all,
A gift of vision you have helped to restore.

The blade of grass, now to count,
The beauty of a baby's face, so bright.
The guiding of your life is of God,
So, in my eyes you are a star.

The new vision, now to enjoy,
The dance of the honey bee to see.
The dance and skillful escape
Of the hummingbird to absorb.

Colors so bright
Butterflies to enjoy
And a heart filled with joy.

I Am Beautiful Give Me A Chance

Black and white all in conflict
Living together with much unrest
Stop the fuss and all the abuse
Our world is made of different hues
We're here together and can't disappear
God's creation made as he saw fit
Forget the color, 'tis skin deep
Let's love each other as Jesus said
The world is made of different colors and hues
Red, yellow, black, brown and white
Are all precious in God's sight
Rainbow of colors and a sky of blue
Makes us one bouquet of a variety of blooms
Let's live, love and sing
No matter the color of the skin
Color fills a world with life
Wish to enjoy it, don't make it sad
We're her same amount of years
In death, same under six feet
We're here a moment in time
Please, to me, be kind.
My life is a weaving
The color I don't choose
The dark threads were as needful
As the gold and silver hues
Man sees my upper side
But God sees my underneath
Please look at me through my inner being
And see me through your heart

What Makes One A Star

The beauty from within and not from without
The humble spirit and not the proud
The love one can give to another hungry heart.
A smile we share with those we love
A kind word to share with those pained.
The lonely to visit and a time to share
The sick to care for and love to show
The hungry to feed and shelter to find
To be a tower for the weak to lean on
To remember and not forget one's humble past
To help the stray one, and bring him home.
To clothe the naked and keep him warm.
To feed the hungry and fill his belly.
That makes for a star.

Heros, A Whisper of Good Will

Ones who love the unlovely give of their time
To visit the sick, the maimed, the lonely and shut-ins
And open a door to let their sun in
Not those who win beauty contests,
Outward beauty will change,
But one who silently serves mankind in need
Being unrecognized in his service
Not the award-winning movie actors, they are only actors
But one who gives the poor
And gives of his need to help those in need
Not the wealthy who give a bit of their surplus
To make a lasting name for themselves
But one who sees the plight of the homeless
And provides an open door, a place to sleep,
And to keep warm
And not the one who shot up in space
In search of God's throne
But one who gives his life to save others
And lose it in the process of saving one
And not the winners of the Nobel Peace Prize
It's those having compassion, helping the poor,
Visiting the prisoners, those who left a falling
Soul and mend the broken hearts
Without those qualities I am
A "sounding brass and tingling cymbal."
Those who are not considered heros
They will silence the world by the whisper of their good will.

Dedicated to All the Lonely and Forgotten

Sometimes it seems like no one cares
Sitting alone, staring out there
Families and loved ones have all but disappeared
Friends must have forgotten me
Here alone living with fear
I call, no one seems to hear
Seems to be falling on deaf ears
Can one open a door for me
To let the sun's rays come in
Just lonely and yearn to be found
Perhaps a little music, a healing sound
Sun rays hidden above the clouds
Musis is silent to my ears
In the face of death, I'll comfortably embrace her
She alone desires my company.

Peace and Prosperity?

In the midst of peace and prosperity,
From within a war goes on
Immorality soaring out of control
Children kidnapped, raped and never seen again
The homeless filling up the streets
Unsafe in schools, fear lurks in the streets
Disgrace to a country, prosperity, rich
In days gone by t'was not so good people walked around
Now filled with those who cheat, steal,
Lie, deceive, and kill
Our society spoiled and gone to sour
Our department stores with bait of 10% discounts
Lure to get my one hundred and 1000
Remember sweet talk is a mouth full of stones
It causes one to stumble and fall
Telemarketing with their sweet talk,
Search out to steal my money
Poison does come out of the snake's mouth
Endless taxing, federal tax, state tax,
City tax, county tax, property tax,
Occupational tax, food tax, gas tax, tax for goods
Taxing my life away, it's a free country
I labor, I pay by the skin of my teeth
Have none left in the bank for me
I wish for peace of mind
In a far away land

The Boy Elian Gonzales

I wish my God-given right
To be home with my dad
Don't buy me with toys
Don't lure me with clothes
To buy me with good times and Disneyland
Make for unjust and false balance
The world is filled with children poor
And the misunderstanding of government
Let's take them all from their parents
You think this makes it right
To be poor it is not a crime
I wish for my common right tonight
To go home and be with my dad
No one has the right to keep us apart
Solomon the wise gave a mother her child
A just weight is God's delight
When I become a man and no longer a child
I'll think as a man and if I wish, I'll soon come back
Don't deprive me from my dad for now
I wish not to be orphaned from dad

Teaching of Tender Years

And the carving of a young heart
TVs and game rooms, sex and crime
Violent cartoons and monstrous toys
Are molding our children's hearts and minds
To the gutters we're dragging them down
Children's innocence is gone
They're carrying knives and guns
Killing sisters, brothers, dads and moms
When committing the crimes, then we're surprised
In his tender years violent cartoons taught him that
Don't be surprised when he commits the crime
Intelligent society has taught him that
The teachings of a child is like carving on a stone
With violence, we're carving the children's hearts
So now forever imputed in their minds
When a child asks for privacy at home
You better know behind his door it's a secrecy
Our children are violated and robbed
Of their good behavior rights
While Hollywood gains fame and racks all the loot
We have need to search the wisdom of Solomon
PR 22:6 Train up a child in the way he should go
When he is old he shall not depart from it
My son, the trouble with thee 'tis with me.

Man a Shadow Soon to Pass

A birth, a cry, a sound of life
Traveling through the birth canal
What great pain was there
Never to be explained
Infants cannot tell
Left helpless on others care
Life bids him welcome with gifts
Of struggle and pain
His days will be few
Storm and tears will meet him
A day will come
When the strong will bow themselves
The grinding will be few and cease
Those which look out of the window will grow dim
The silver cords will be loose
His years will come near to a close
Evil day will come there'll be no pleasure in them
Fear will visit and be in the way
The sound of music will be brought low, desire will fail
He fold up to his fetal shape once more
He goes to his long home
Death will embrace
No longer remembered,
His dust will return to the earth
"What profeteth a man
To gain a world and lose his soul"
Man is vanity, his days are shadows will pass away

Let Me Do Good

If I may do good, let me do it now
For I'll not pass this way again
Let me be the coal of fire that glows
To warm the lonely hearts
For tomorrow my glow shall die
Let me speak kind words, keep truth in my lips,
Carry charity in my hands.
Have compassion and love in my eyes,
Uprightness in my walk,
Pray for those I dislike.
Let love dwell in my heart towards all
Let me not turn my eyes when I see a wounded soul,
But turn with tenderness toward him with help
If I may do good, let me do it now
For I'll not pass this way again
I'll not pass for tomorrow what I can do today,
But turn my eyes to focus on tomorrow's darkness
Where I could stumble in today's lights
Let me be the coal of fire to keep warm,
The hearts of all who cross my path
For tomorrow my glow shall translate to dust
If I may do good, let me do it now
For I shall not pass this way again.

Back Then

Tata, tell me about when you were a little girl
Grandson, those were the lovely years
Beginning of Truman and the end of Roosevelt
Back then we were unique and we earned it sweet
We were friendly, caring, loving and sharing
We knew our neighbors by name
Children went out to play and were not afraid
We washed our clothes by hand
We hung them out on the lines
An art today we've lost
Our diapers were made of cloth
We had no locks on our doors
We went to sleep with open doors
We sat outside on screened, covered porches
We did our shopping in a Five and Ten cents store
We could not wear out those clothes
Fathers went to work, Mothers stayed home
Postmen brought our mail to our door
He blew the whistle and delivered mail by hand
From him we bought our two and three cent stamps
We milked our cows and drank it on the spot
And the cream floated on the top
We killed our hogs for ham and souse
We hang the ham out in the smokehouse
Raised chickens for homemade eggs
Made homemade quilts with love and care
We read the Bible in schools
We had prayers in school to boot
Winter nights we froze to death
For there was no central heat
We snuggled under two and three quilts
We were happy and satisfied

Morning, we froze to death
Till we got out fireplace to start
Cars were used for pleasure rides
A gallon of gas for 25 cents
Movies were outdoors
Kids didn't carry guns
And respected parent, grandmas and all
Friends walked in, nothing we feared
Now I and my things we've become antiques
Filled with beauty and wisdom's reasoning
Unique and of a valuable prize

All Is Vanity

All humanity love to welcome the newborn
The old put aside undesired, and society wishes them gone
A day will come, this moment in time to all
Man will shed off his beauty, strength,
Characteristic, personality and knowledge
When the strong shall bow themselves
The grinders will cease, for they'll be few
Those which look out of windows will grow dim
The doors in the streets shall be shut
All desires of men will fail, be gone
The sound of music shall be made low
Man will be afraid of that which is high
Constantly, fear shall be in the way
And he goes to his long home, from whence he came
Dust will return to earth as it was
The spirit of men shall return to God who gave it
Then the eyes of men be filled with a hand of dust
In his grave man will be belly full, satisfied and content
Remember your Creator in the days of strength and youth
Before the evil day comes and years draws near
And have no pleasure in them
Man is grass, his days are numbered
And swiftly passing, all is vanity
Like the flowers than come up and are cut down
Man is born of a woman
Is of few days and full of troubles.

Vanishing Race

Superiority and greed overtakes the simple
And the innocent perish
Movements of a bush, a whisk of a branch
White men lurking behind, man from a far away land
Bearing gifts of death, a stumbling stone to my path,
The red man to kill, their land to possess
A dark cloud hovering above, a future promising darkness
My lights are dim
My days are numbered and are swiftly passing
My warriors bowed to their knees
Hunted, wounded game left to die
I search a ray of hope, darkness I find
The eagle no longer soars, the broken wing his reward
Ethnic cleansed the country of me
To a desolate land they left me
Uprooted from my land, all hope is gone
Stripped of my land, my pride, my right, my life
My hunting ground they have taken
My buffalo slaughtered in their fields
In the darkest hour the wolf howls, the ancient of my day
The hawks call falls silent to my ears
My eagle is taken for their symbol is taken
The sun will not rise over the horizon
My eyes will no longer behold
The piercing of the morning sun's rays
Stripped and wounded game, I die
The mighty one has fallen, the crown broken
I am left to be searched for in pages of history
A nation erased, forever gone
To be remembered a nation of the past
And we dare say all men are created equal.

To Absorb a Beauty in Life

I wish not the fast life
I care not to my grave run
Soon death will meet face to face
We shall comfortably each other embrace
I'll not race to meet her now
I rather smell the rose and daffodils
The fireflies light up and sparkle my space
And to watch birds fly in the air
At the break of dawn, listening to the bird's songs
And observe the fluttering of a humming bird dance in space
And to go out fields, dancing freely around the flower beds
At dusk, spreading my bed under heaven, I count the stars
To consider the moon, the stars,
To marvel at the handy work and creations of God
To observe a creation beautifully designed by God's hands
For the pleasing of mankind
I'll search to delight myself in that which God mad perfect
For the good of man
I'll spend my day listening to the laughter of babes
And catch that breath of air and thank my God for that day
If I were an eagle, I'd soar the heavens
High above the clouds to absorb all the beauty
Of the handy work of God from above
I'll observe the sun, casting her gold threads down the river runs,
I'll glide down the river run to drink my fill,
And to satisfy my thirsty soul
I wish to miss none of it for this portion is mine,
To live, to enjoy

I'll not race across dark paved highways
Racing my life away
To be reminded of dark, gloomy days
I'll not wait for tomorrow's rain, I'll dance in my sun today
For the things man makes are in themselves
Imperfect and vain, and lacking of spirit
For that which now is in days to come
It shall be forgotten
And how dieth the wise and the fool
It is God who gives life, wisdom, knowledge and joy
And to every thing a turn.